God's Beautiful World

Lord our Lord,
how excellent is thy name
in all the earth!

Psalm 8:1

IDEALS PUBLISHING CORPORATION
NASHVILLE, TENNESSEE

PHOTOGRAPHS

Cover, FPG; **4-5**, FPG; **6**, Gay Bumgarner; **8-9**, Johnson's Photography; **10-11**, Dianne Dietrich Leis; **12-13**, FPG; **14**, Johnson's Photography; **16-17**, FPG; **18-19**, Daniel E. Dempster; **20-21**, Dianne Dietrich Leis; **22**, Gay Bumgarner; **25**, FPG; **26-27**, Gene Ahrens; **29**, Dianne Dietrich Leis; **30**, Johnson's Photography; **33**, Johnson's Photography; **34-35**, Johnson's Photography; **37**, Gene Ahrens; **39**, Ed Cooper; **40-41**, FPG; **42-43**, Johnson's Photography; **44-45**, Adam Jones; **46-47**, FPG; **48-49**, FPG; **50**, Ed Cooper; **52-53**, Gay Bumgarner; **54-55**, Daniel E. Dempster; **56**, Gene Ahrens; **58**, Ed Cooper; **60-61**, Sherrie Jones; **62**, Adam Jones; **64**, Gay Bumgarner; **66-67**, Adam Jones; **68-69**, Adam Jones; **70-71**, FPG; **73**, Sherrie Jones; **74-75**, FPG; **77**, Johnson's Photography; **78-79**, FPG; **80-81**, Gay Bumgarner; **82-83**, Adam Jones; **84-85**, FPG; **86**, Daniel E. Dempster; **89**, Adam Jones; **90-91**, Johnson's Photography; **92**, Gay Bumgarner; **94-95**, Gay Bumgarner; **96**, Sherrie Jones; **98**, Gay Bumgarner; **100-101**, Dianne Dietrich Leis; **102**, Gay Bumgarner; **104-105**, Gay Bumgarner; **107**, Gay Bumgarner; **108**, Adam Jones; **110-11**, Gene Ahrens; **112**, Ed Cooper; **114-115**, FPG; **116-117**, Gene Ahrens; **118**, Daniel E. Dempster; **120-121**, FPG; **122**, Adam Jones; **125**, Adam Jones; **127**, Adam Jones; **129**, Johnson's Photography; **131**, FPG; **132**, Adam Jones; **134-135**, FPG; **136-137**, Adam Jones; **139**, Johnson's Photography; **140-141**, Johnson's Photography; **142**, Adam Jones; **144**, Johnson's Photography; **146**, Adam Jones; **148**, Johnson's Photography; **150-151**, Daniel E. Dempster; **153**, Adam Jones; **154**, Daniel E. Dempster; **156-157**, Adam Jones; **158-159**, FPG.

Printed and bound in the U. S. A.

ISBN 0-8249-4052-0

Film separations by Precision Color Graphics

Cover type Shelley Allegro; text type Cochin Italic Light

Publisher, Patricia A. Pingry; Editor, Nancy J. Skarmeas; Art Director, Patrick T. McRae; Copy Editor, Laura Matter

Contents

The Glory
of God

The heavens
declare
the glory
of God;
and the
firmament
sheweth his
handywork.

Psalm 19:1

Give ear to my words, O Lord, consider my meditation. Hearken unto the voice of my cry, my King, and my God: for unto thee will I pray. My voice shalt thou hear in the morning, O Lord; in the morning will I direct my prayer unto thee, and will look up. . . . I will come into thy house in the multitude of thy mercy: and in thy fear will I worship toward thy holy temple. Lead me, O Lord, in thy righteousness because of mine enemies; make thy way straight before my face. . . . let all those that put their trust in thee rejoice: let them ever shout for joy, because thou defendest them: let them also that love thy name be joyful in thee. For thou, Lord, wilt bless the righteous; with favour wilt thou compass him as with a shield.

Psalm 5: 1-3; 7; 8; 11; 12

he Lord reigneth;
let the earth
rejoice; let the multitude of
isles be glad thereof.
Clouds and darkness
are round about him:
righteousness and judgment are
the habitation of his throne. . . .
The heavens declare his
righteousness, and all
the people see his glory. . . .
Light is sown for the righteous,
and gladness for the upright
in heart. Rejoice in the Lord,
ye righteous; and give thanks
at the remembrance
of his holiness.

Psalm 97: 1; 2; 6; 11; 12

 lessed be thou,
Lord God of Israel
our father, for ever and ever.
Thine, O Lord, is the greatness,
and the power, and the glory,
and the victory, and the majesty:
for all that is in the heaven and
in the earth is thine; thine is
the kingdom, O Lord, and thou
art exalted as head above all.
Both riches and honour come
of thee, and thou reignest over all;
and in thine hand is power and
might; and in thine hand it is
to make great, and to give
strength unto all. Now
therefore, our God, we thank thee,
and praise thy glorious name.

I Chronicles 29: 10-13

**A**nd God said,
Let there be lights
in the firmament of the heaven
to divide the day from the night; and
let them be for signs, and for seasons,
and for days, and years: And let them be
for lights in the firmament of the heaven
to give light upon the earth: and it was so.
And God made two great lights; the
greater light to rule the day,
and the lesser light to rule the night: he
made the stars also. And God set them
in the firmament of the heaven to give
light upon the earth, And to rule over
the day and over the night, and to divide
the light from the darkness:
and God saw that it was good.

Genesis 1: 14-18

I will praise thee with my whole heart: before the gods will I sing praise unto thee. I will worship toward thy holy temple, and praise thy name for thy lovingkindness and for thy truth: for thou hast magnified thy word above all thy name. In the day when I cried thou answeredst me, and strengthenedst me with strength in my soul. All the kings of the earth shall praise thee, O Lord, when they hear the words of thy mouth. Yea, they shall sing in the ways of the Lord: for great is the glory of the Lord. Though the Lord be high, yet hath he respect unto the lowly: but the proud he knoweth afar off. Though I walk in the midst of trouble, thou wilt revive me: thou shalt stretch forth thine hand . . . and thy right hand shall save me. The Lord will perfect that which concerneth me: thy mercy, O Lord, endureth for ever: forsake not the works of thine own hands.

Psalm 138

*O come, let us sing
unto the Lord: let us
make a joyful noise to the rock of
our salvation. Let us come before
his presence with thanksgiving,
and make a joyful noise unto him
with psalms. For the Lord is
a great God, and a great King
above all gods. In his hand are
the deep places of the earth: the
strength of the hills is his also.
The sea is his, and he made it: and
his hands formed the dry land.
O come, let us worship and bow down:
let us kneel before the Lord our maker.
For he is our God; and we are the
people of his pasture, and
the sheep of his hand.*

Psalm 95: 1-7

give thanks unto
the Lord; for he is good:
for his mercy endureth for ever. O give thanks
unto the God of gods: for his mercy endureth
for ever. O give thanks to the Lord of lords:
for his mercy endureth for ever. To him who
alone doeth great wonders: for his mercy
endureth for ever. To him that by wisdom
made the heavens: for his mercy endureth
for ever. To him that stretched out the earth
above the waters: for his mercy endureth
for ever. To him that made great lights:
for his mercy endureth for ever: The sun to rule
by day: for his mercy endureth for ever:
The moon and stars to rule by night:
for his mercy endureth for ever. . . .
O give thanks unto the God of heaven:
for his mercy endureth for ever.

Psalm 136: 1-9; 26

THE GLORY OF GOD

O sing unto the Lord
a new song: sing unto
the Lord, all the earth. Sing unto
the Lord, bless his name; shew forth
his salvation from day to day.
Declare his glory among the heathen,
his wonders among all people.
For the Lord is great, and greatly
to be praised: he is to be feared above
all gods. For all the gods of the nations
are idols: but the Lord made
the heavens. Honour and majesty are
before him: strength and beauty
are in his sanctuary.

Psalm 96: 1-6

God's Beautiful World

will extol thee, my God, O king; and I will bless thy name for ever and ever. Every day will I bless thee; and I will praise thy name for ever and ever. Great is the Lord, and greatly to be praised; and his greatness is unsearchable. One generation shall praise thy works to another, and shall declare thy mighty acts. I will speak of the glorious honour of thy majesty, and of thy wondrous works. And men shall speak of the might of thy terrible acts: and I will declare thy greatness. They shall abundantly utter the memory of thy great goodness, and shall sing of thy righteousness.

Psalm 145: 1-7

The heavens declare the glory of God; and the firmament sheweth his handywork. Day unto day uttereth speech, and night unto night sheweth knowledge. There is no speech nor language, where their voice is not heard. Their line is gone out through all the earth, and their words to the end of the world. In them hath he set a tabernacle for the sun, Which is as a bridegroom coming out of his chamber, and rejoiceth as a strong man to run a race. His going forth is from the end of the heaven, and his circuit unto the ends of it: and there is nothing hid from the heat thereof. The law of the Lord is perfect, converting the soul: the testimony of the Lord is sure, making wise the simple. The statutes of the Lord are right, rejoicing the heart: the commandment of the Lord is pure, enlightening the eyes. The fear of the Lord is clean, enduring for ever: the judgments of the Lord are true and righteous altogether. More to be desired are they than gold, yea, than much fine gold: sweeter also than honey. . . . Let the words of my mouth, and the meditation of my heart, be acceptable in thy sight, O Lord, my strength, and my redeemer.

Psalm 19: 1-10; 14

Our
Dwelling Place

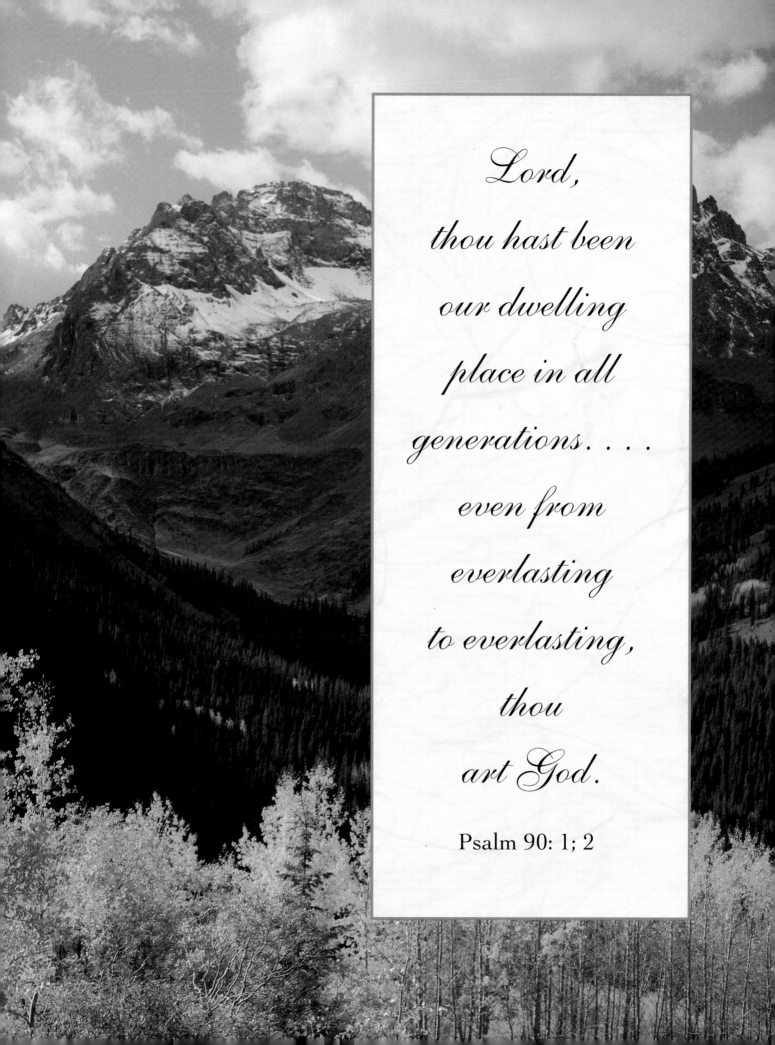

*Lord,
thou hast been
our dwelling
place in all
generations. . . .
even from
everlasting
to everlasting,
thou
art God.*

Psalm 90: 1; 2

ruly my soul waiteth upon God:
from him cometh my salvation.

He only is my rock and my salvation; he is my defence;

I shall not be greatly moved. . . . My soul, wait thou only upon

God; for my expectation is from him. He only is my rock

and my salvation: he is my defence; I shall not be moved.

In God is my salvation and my glory: the rock of my strength,

and my refuge, is in God. Trust in him at all times: ye people,

pour out your heart before him: God is a refuge for us.

Surely men of low degree are vanity, and men of high degree

are a lie: to be laid in the balance, they are altogether lighter

than vanity. Trust not in oppression, and become not vain

in robbery: if riches increase, set not your heart upon them.

God hath spoken once; twice have I heard this; that power

belongeth unto God. Also unto thee, O Lord,

belongeth mercy: for thou renderest to every man

according to his work.

Psalm 62: 1; 2; 5-12

**I**n thee, O Lord, do I put my trust; let me never be ashamed: deliver me in thy righteousness. Bow down thine ear to me; deliver me speedily: Be thou my strong rock, for an house of defence to save me. For thou art my rock and my fortress; therefore for thy name's sake lead me, and guide me. Pull me out of the net that they have laid privily for me: for thou art my strength. Into thine hand I commit my spirit: thou hast redeemed me, O Lord God of truth. . . . O love the Lord, all ye his saints: for the Lord preserveth the faithful, and plentifully rewardeth the proud doer. Be of good courage, and he shall strengthen your heart, all ye that hope in the Lord.

Psalm 31: 1-5; 23; 24

The earth is the Lord's, and the fulness thereof; the world, and they that dwell therein. For he hath founded it upon the seas, and established it upon the floods. Who shall ascend into the hill of the Lord? or who shall stand in his holy place? He that hath clean hands, and a pure heart; who hath not lifted up his soul into vanity, nor sworn deceitfully. He shall receive the blessing from the Lord, and righteousness from the God of his salvation. . . .

Lift up your heads, O ye gates; and be ye lift up, ye everlasting doors; and the King of glory shall come in. Who is this King of glory? The Lord strong and mighty, the Lord mighty in battle. Lift up your heads, O ye gates; even lift them up, ye everlasting doors; and the King of glory shall come in. Who is the King of glory? The Lord of hosts, he is the King of glory.

Psalm 24: 1-5; 7-10

**I** will lift up mine eyes unto the hills, from whence cometh my help. My help cometh from the Lord, which made heaven and earth. He will not suffer thy foot to be moved: he that keepeth thee will not slumber. Behold, he that keepeth Israel shall neither slumber nor sleep. The Lord is thy keeper: the Lord is thy shade upon thy right hand. The sun shall not smite thee by day, nor the moon by night. The Lord shall preserve thee from all evil: he shall preserve thy soul. The Lord shall preserve thy going out and thy coming in from this time forth, and even for evermore.

Psalm 121

Teach me, O Lord, the way of thy statutes; and I shall keep it unto the end. Give me understanding, and I shall keep thy law; yea, I shall observe it with my whole heart. Make me to go in the path of thy commandments; for therein do I delight. Incline my heart unto thy testimonies, and not to covetousness. Turn away mine eyes from beholding vanity; and quicken thou me in thy way. Stablish thy word unto thy servant, who is devoted to thy fear. Turn away my reproach which I fear: for thy judgments are good. Behold, I have longed after thy precepts: quicken me in thy righteousness.

Psalm 119: 33-40

I will love thee, O Lord, my strength. The Lord is my rock, and my fortress, and my deliverer; my God, my strength, in whom I will trust; my buckler, and the horn of my salvation, and my high tower. . . . In my distress I called upon the Lord, and cried unto my God: he heard my voice out of his temple, and my cry came before him, even into his ears. . . . He brought me forth also into a large place; he delivered me, because he delighted in me. . . . With the merciful thou wilt shew thyself merciful; with an upright man thou wilt shew thyself upright; With the pure thou wilt shew thyself pure; and with the froward thou wilt shew thyself froward. For thou wilt save the afflicted people; but wilt bring down high looks. For thou wilt light my candle: the Lord my God will enlighten my darkness. For by thee I have run through a troop; and by my God have I leaped over a wall. As for God, his way is perfect: the word of the Lord is tried: he is a buckler to all those that trust in him. For who is God save the Lord? or who is a rock save our God? It is God that girdeth me with strength, and maketh my way perfect. He maketh my feet like hinds' feet, and setteth me upon my high places. . . . The Lord liveth; and blessed be my rock; and let the God of my salvation be exalted.

Psalm 18: 1; 2; 6; 19; 25-33; 46

*L*ord, who shall abide
in thy tabernacle?
who shall dwell upon thy holy hill?
He that walketh uprightly, and
worketh righteousness, and speaketh
the truth in his heart. He that backbiteth
not with his tongue, nor doeth evil
to his neighbour, nor taketh up a
reproach against his neighbour.
In whose eyes a vile person is
contemned; but he honoureth them
that fear the Lord. He that sweareth
to his own hurt, and changeth not.
He that putteth not out his money
to usury, nor taketh reward
against the innocent. He that doeth
these things shall never be moved.

Psalm 15

od is our refuge and strength, a very present help in trouble. Therefore will not we fear; though the earth be removed, and though the mountains be carried into the midst of the sea; Though the waters thereof roar and be troubled, though the mountains shake with the swelling thereof. There is a river, the streams whereof shall make glad the city of God, the holy place of the tabernacles of the most High. God is in the midst of her; she shall not be moved: God shall help her; and that right early. . . . Be still, and know that I am God: I will be exalted among the heathen, I will be exalted in the earth.

Psalm 46: 1-5; 10

ehold, God is mighty,
and despiseth not any:
he is mighty in strength and wisdom.
He preserveth not the life of the wicked:
but giveth right to the poor. He withdraweth
not his eyes from the righteous: but with
kings are they on the throne; yea, he doth
establish them for ever, and they are exalted.
And if they be bound in fetters, and
be holden in cords of affliction; Then he
sheweth them their work, and their
transgressions that they have exceeded.
He openeth also their ear to discipline,
and commandeth that they return from
iniquity. If they obey and serve him,
they shall spend their days in prosperity,
and their years in pleasures.

Job 36: 5-11

H

e that dwelleth
in the secret place
of the most High shall abide under
the shadow of the Almighty.
I will say of the Lord,
He is my refuge and my fortress:
my God; in him will I trust.
Surely he shall deliver thee from
the snare of the fowler,
and from the noisome pestilence.
He shall cover thee with
his feathers, and under his wings
shalt thou trust:
his truth shall be thy shield
and buckler.

Psalm 91: 1-4

The Still
Waters

He leadeth
me beside
the still
waters.
He restoreth
my soul.

Psalm 23: 2; 3

G od, thou art my God;
early will I seek thee: my soul
thirsteth for thee, my flesh longeth for thee in a dry
and thirsty land, where no water is; To see thy power and
thy glory, so as I have seen thee in the sanctuary.
Because thy lovingkindness is better than life,
my lips shall praise thee. Thus will I bless thee
while I live: I will lift up my hands in my name.
My soul shall be satisfied as with marrow and fatness;
and my mouth shall praise thee with joyful lips:
When I remember thee upon my bed, and meditate on thee
in the night watches. Because thou hast been my help,
therefore in the shadow of thy wings will I rejoice.
My soul followeth hard after thee:
thy right hand upholdeth me.

Psalm 63: 1-8

Rejoice in the Lord alway: and again I say, Rejoice. Let your moderation be known unto all men. The Lord is at hand. Be careful for nothing; but in every thing by prayer and supplication with thanksgiving let your requests be made known unto God. And the peace of God, which passeth all understanding, shall keep your hearts and minds through Christ Jesus.

Philippians 4: 4-7

In those days came John the Baptist,
preaching in the wilderness of Judea,
and saying, Repent ye: for the kingdom of heaven is
at hand. . . . I indeed baptize you with water unto
repentance: but he that cometh after me is mightier than
I, whose shoes I am not worthy to bear: he shall
baptize you with the Holy Ghost, and with fire. . . .
Then cometh Jesus from Galilee to Jordan unto John,
to be baptized of him. But John forbad him, saying,
I have need to be baptized of thee, and comest thou to me?
And Jesus answering said unto him, Suffer it to be so
now: for thus it becometh us to fulfil all righteousness.
Then he suffered him. And Jesus, when he was baptized,
went up straightway out of the water: and, lo,
the heavens were opened unto him, and he saw
the Spirit of God descending like a dove, and lighting
upon him: And lo a voice from heaven, saying, This
is my beloved Son, in whom I am well pleased.

Matthew 3: 1; 2; 11; 13-17

ave mercy upon me, O God,

according to thy lovingkindness:

according unto the multitude of thy tender mercies blot out

my transgressions. Wash me thoroughly from mine iniquity,

and cleanse me from my sin. . . . Purge me with hyssop,

and I shall be clean: wash me, and I shall be whiter than snow.

Make me to hear joy and gladness; that the bones which

thou hast broken may rejoice. . . . Create in me a clean heart,

O God; and renew a right spirit within me. Cast me not

away from thy presence; and take not thy holy spirit from me.

Restore unto me the joy of thy salvation;

and uphold me with thy free spirit. . . . O Lord, open thou my lips;

and my mouth shall shew forth thy praise.

Psalm 51: 1; 2; 7; 8; 10-12; 15

Bless the Lord, O my soul. O Lord my God, thou art very great; thou art clothed with honour and majesty. Who coverest thyself with light as with a garment: who stretchest out the heavens like a curtain: Who layeth the beams of his chambers in the waters: who maketh the clouds his chariot: who walketh upon the wings of the wind: Who maketh his angels spirits; his ministers a flaming fire: Who laid the foundations of the earth, that it should not be removed for ever. Thou coveredst it with the deep as with a garment: the waters stood above the mountains. At thy rebuke they fled; at the voice of thy thunder they hasted away. They go up by the mountains; they go down by the valleys unto the place which thou hast founded for them. Thou hast set a bound that they may not pass over; that they turn not again to cover the earth.

Psalm 104: 1-9

Cast thy bread upon the waters: for thou shalt find it after many days. Give a portion to seven, and also to eight; for thou knowest not what evil shall be upon the earth. If the clouds be full of rain, they empty themselves upon the earth: and if the tree fall toward the south, or toward the north, in the place where the tree falleth, there it shall be. He that observeth the wind shall not sow; and he that regardeth the clouds shall not reap. As thou knowest not what is the way of the spirit, nor how the bones do grow in the womb of her that is with child: even so thou knowest not the works of God who maketh all.

Ecclesiastes 11: 1-5

s the hart panteth after the water brooks,
so panteth my soul after thee, O God.
My soul thirsteth for God, for the living God: when shall I come
and appear before God? My tears have been my meat day and night,
while they continually say unto me, Where is thy God? When I
remember these things, I pour out my soul in me: for I had gone
with the multitude, I went with them to the house of God,
with the voice of joy and praise, with a multitude that kept holyday.
Why art thou cast down, O my soul? and why art thou disquieted
in me? hope thou in God: for I shall yet praise him for the help of his
countenance. O my God, my soul is cast down within me:
therefore will I remember thee. . . . Deep calleth unto deep at the noise
of thy waterspouts: all thy waves and thy billows are gone over me.
Yet the Lord will command his lovingkindness in the daytime,
and in the night his song shall be with me, and my prayer unto
the God of my life. . . . Why art thou cast down, O my soul?
and why art thou disquieted within me? hope thou in God:
for I shall yet praise him, who is the health
of my countenance, and my God.

Psalm 42: 1-8; 11

Unto thee, O Lord, do I lift up my soul.
O my God, I trust in thee: let me not be
ashamed, let not mine enemies triumph over me. Yea, let none
that wait on thee be ashamed: let them be ashamed which
transgress without cause. Shew me thy ways, O Lord; teach me
thy paths. Lead me in thy truth, and teach me: for thou art the
God of my salvation; on thee do I wait all the day. Remember,
O Lord, thy tender mercies and the lovingkindnesses;
for they have been ever of old. Remember not the sins of my youth,
nor my transgressions: according to thy mercy remember thou me
for thy goodness' sake, O Lord. Good and upright is the Lord:
therefore will he teach sinners in the way. The meek will he guide
in judgment: and the meek will he teach his way. All the paths
of the Lord are mercy and truth unto such as keep his
covenant and his testimonies. . . . O keep my soul, and deliver me:
let me not be ashamed; for I put my trust in thee.
Let integrity and uprightness preserve me;
for I wait on thee.

Psalm 25: 1-10; 20; 21

Give unto the Lord, O ye mighty, give unto the Lord glory and strength. Give unto the Lord the glory due unto his name; worship the Lord in the beauty of holiness. The voice of the Lord is upon the waters: the God of glory thundereth: the Lord is upon many waters. The voice of the Lord is powerful; the voice of the Lord is full of majesty. . . . The voice of the Lord maketh the hinds to calve, and discovereth the forests: and in his temple doth every one speak his glory. The Lord sitteth upon the flood; yea, the Lord sitteth King for ever. The Lord will give strength unto his people; the Lord will bless his people with peace.

Psalm 29: 1-4; 9-11

**T**he Lord is my shepherd;
I shall not want.
He maketh me to lie down
in green pastures: he leadeth me beside
the still waters. He restoreth my soul:
he leadeth me in the paths
of righteousness for his name's sake.
Yea, though I walk through the valley
of the shadow of death, I will fear
no evil: for thou art with me; thy rod
and thy staff they comfort me. Thou
preparest a table before me in the
presence of mine enemies: thou
anointest my head with oil; my cup
runneth over. Surely goodness and mercy
shall follow me all the days of my life:
and I will dwell in the house
of the Lord for ever.

Psalm 23

The Lilies
of the Field

Consider
the lilies
of the field,
how
they grow;
they toil not,
neither
do they spin.

Matthew 6: 28b

Praise waiteth for thee, O God. . . .

Thou visitest the earth, and waterest it:

thou greatly enrichest it with the river of God,

which is full of water: thou preparest them corn,

when thou hast so provided for it. Thou waterest the ridges

thereof abundantly: thou settlest the furrows thereof:

thou makest it soft with showers: thou blessest the

springing thereof. Thou crownest the year with thy goodness;

and thy paths drop fatness. They drop upon the pastures

of the wilderness: and the little hills rejoice on every side.

The pastures are clothed with flocks;

the valleys also are covered over with corn;

they shout for joy, they also sing.

Psalm 65: 1; 9-13

onsider the lilies of
the field, how they grow;
they toil not, neither do they spin.
And yet I say unto you, That even Solomon
in all his glory was not arrayed like one
of these. Wherefore, if God so clothe the
grass of the field, which to day is,
and to morrow is cast into the oven,
shall he not much more clothe you,
O ye of little faith? Therefore take no
thought, saying, What shall we eat? or,
What shall we drink? or, Wherewithal
shall we be clothed? . . . for your heavenly
Father knoweth that ye have need of all these
things. But seek ye first the kingdom
of God, and his righteousness; and all these
things shall be added unto you. Take
therefore no thought for the morrow:
for the morrow shall take thought
for the things of itself.

Matthew 6: 28-34

For the Lord thy God bringeth
thee into a good land, a land of brooks
of water, of fountains and depths that spring
out of valleys and hills; A land of wheat, and barley,
and vines, and fig trees, and pomegranates;
a land of oil olive, and honey; A land wherein thou
shalt eat bread without scarceness,
thou shalt not lack any thing in it;
a land whose stones are iron,
and out of whose hills thou
mayest dig brass.

Deuteronomy 8: 7-9

*S*ing unto the Lord,
all the earth; shew forth
from day to day his salvation. Declare
his glory. . . . Glory and honour are
in his presence; strength and gladness
are in his place. Give unto the Lord,
ye kindreds of the people, give unto the
Lord glory and strength. Give unto
the Lord the glory due unto his name:
bring an offering, and come before him:
worship the Lord in the beauty
of holiness. . . . Let the heavens
be glad, and let the earth rejoice: and
let men say among the nations, The Lord
reigneth. Let the sea roar, and the fulness
thereof: let the fields rejoice, and all that is
therein. Then shall the trees of the wood
sing out at the presence of the Lord. . . .
O give thanks unto the Lord; for he is
good; for his mercy endureth for ever.

I Chronicles 16: 23; 24; 27-29; 31-34

Let the heavens rejoice, and let the earth be glad; let the sea roar, and the fulness thereof. Let the field be joyful, and all that is therein: then shall all the trees of the wood rejoice Before the Lord: for he cometh, for he cometh to judge the earth: he shall judge the world with righteousness, and the people with his truth.

Psalm 96: 11-13

THE LILIES OF THE FIELD

omfort ye, comfort ye my
people, saith your God. . . .
The voice of him that crieth in the wilderness,
Prepare ye the way of the Lord, make
straight in the desert a highway for our
God. Every valley shall be exalted,
and every mountain and hill shall be
made low: and the crooked shall be made
straight, and the rough places plain: And
the glory of the Lord shall be revealed, and
all flesh shall see it together: for the
mouth of the Lord hath spoken it. The
voice said, Cry. And he said, What shall
I cry? All flesh is grass, and all the
goodliness thereof is as the flower of the field:
The grass withereth, the flower fadeth:
because the spirit of the Lord bloweth upon it:
surely the people is grass. The grass withereth,
the flower fadeth: but the word
of our God shall stand for ever.

Isaiah 40: 1; 3-8

**A**sk, and it shall be given you; seek, and ye shall find; knock, and it shall be opened. . . . Or what man is there of you, whom if his son ask bread, will he give him a stone? Or if he ask a fish, will he give him a serpent? If ye then, being evil, know how to give good gifts unto your children, how much more shall your Father which is in heaven give good things to them that ask him?

Matthew 7: 7; 9-11

Have mercy upon me, O God,
according to thy lovingkindness:
according unto the multitude of thy tender mercies
blot out my transgressions. Wash me thoroughly from
mine iniquity, and cleanse me from my sin. . . .
Make me to hear joy and gladness; that the bones
which thou hast broken may rejoice. . . .
Create in me a clean heart, O God; and renew
a right spirit within me. Cast me not away from
thy presence; and take not thy holy spirit from me.
Restore unto me the joy of thy salvation;
and uphold me with thy free spirit. . . .
O Lord, open thou my lips; and my mouth
shall shew forth thy praise.

Psalm 51: 1; 2; 8; 10-12; 15

And seeing the multitudes, he went up into
a mountain: and when he was set, his disciples
came unto him: And he opened his mouth, and taught them,
saying, Blessed are the poor in spirit: for theirs is
the kingdom of heaven. Blessed are they that mourn: for they
shall be comforted. Blessed are the meek: for they shall
inherit the earth. Blessed are they which do hunger and thirst
after righteousness: for they shall be filled. Blessed are the merciful:
for they shall obtain mercy. Blessed are the pure in heart:
for they shall see God. Blessed are the peacemakers:
for they shall be called the children of God. Blessed are they which
are persecuted for righteousness' sake: for theirs is
the kingdom of heaven. Blessed are ye, when men shall
revile you, and persecute you, and shall say
all manner of evil against you falsely,
for my sake. Rejoice, and be exceeding glad:
for great is your reward in heaven.

Matthew 5: 1-12

How Manifold
Are Thy Works

O Lord,
how manifold
are thy works!
in wisdom
hast thou
made them all:
the earth
is full of thy
riches.

Psalm 104: 24

GOD'S BEAUTIFUL WORLD

 Lord our Lord, how excellent

is thy name in all the earth!

who hast set thy glory above the heavens. . . .

When I consider thy heavens, the work of thy fingers,

the moon and the stars, which thou hast ordained;

What is man, that thou art mindful of him?

and the son of man, that thou visitest him?

For thou hast made him a little lower than the angels,

and hast crowned him with glory and honour.

Thou madest him to have dominion over the works

of thy hands: thou hast put all things under his feet:

All sheep and oxen, yea, and the beasts of the field;

The fowl of the air, and the fish of the sea,

and whatsoever passeth through the paths of the seas.

O Lord our Lord, how excellent is thy name

in all the earth!

Psalm 8: 1; 3-9

GOD'S BEAUTIFUL WORLD

Praise ye the Lord, Praise ye the Lord from the heavens: praise him in the heights. Praise ye him, all his angels: praise ye him, all his hosts. Praise ye him, sun and moon: praise him, all ye stars of light. Praise him, ye heavens of heavens, and ye waters that be above the heavens. Let them praise the name of the Lord: for he commanded, and they were created. He hath also stablished them for ever and ever: he hath made a decree which shall not pass. Praise the Lord from the earth, ye dragons, and all deeps: Fire, and hail; snow, and vapours; stormy wind fulfilling his word: Mountains, and all hills; fruitful trees, and all cedars: Beasts, and all cattle; creeping things, and flying fowl: Kings of the earth, and all people; princes, and all judges of the earth: Both young men, and maidens; old men, and children: Let them praise the name of the Lord: for his name alone is excellent; his glory is above the earth and heaven. He also exalteth the horn of his people, the praise of all his saints; even of the children of Israel, a people near unto him. Praise ye the Lord.

Psalm 148

For this cause I bow my knees unto the Father of our Lord Jesus Christ, Of whom the whole family in heaven and earth is named, That he would grant you, according to the riches of his glory, to be strengthened with might by his Spirit in the inner man; That Christ may dwell in your hearts by faith; that ye, being rooted and grounded in love, May be able to comprehend with all saints what is the breadth, and length, and depth, and height; And to know the love of Christ, which passeth knowledge, that ye might be filled with all the fulness of God. Now unto him that is able to do exceeding abundantly above all that we ask or think, according to the power that worketh in us, Unto him be glory in the church by Christ Jesus throughout all ages, world without end.

Ephesians 3: 14-21

O Lord, how manifold are thy works!
in wisdom hast thou made them all:
the earth is full of thy riches. So is this great and wide sea,
wherein are things creeping innumerable, both small and
great beasts. There go the ships: there is that leviathan,
whom thou hast made to play therein. These wait all
upon thee; that thou mayest give them their meat in
due season. That thou givest them they gather: thou openest
thine hand, they are filled with good. Thou hidest thy face,
they are troubled: thou takest away their breath, they die,
and return to their dust. Thou sendest forth thy spirit,
they are created: and thou renewest
the face of the earth.

Psalm 104: 24-30

Praise ye the Lord.
I will praise the Lord
with my whole heart, in the assembly
of the upright, and in the congregation.
The works of the Lord are great,
sought out of all them that have
pleasure therein. His work is honourable
and glorious: and his righteousness
endureth for ever. He hath made
his wonderful works to be remembered:
the Lord is gracious and full
of compassion. . . . The works
of his hands are verity and judgment;
all his commandments are sure.
They stand fast for ever and ever,
and are done in truth
and uprightness.

Psalm 111: 1-4; 7; 8

GOD'S BEAUTIFUL WORLD

he Lord is the portion
of mine inheritance and
of my cup: thou maintainest my lot. The lines are fallen
unto me in pleasant places; yea, I have a goodly heritage.
I will bless the Lord, who hath given me counsel:
my reins also instruct me in the night seasons. I have set
the Lord always before me: because he is at my right hand,
I shall not be moved. Therefore my heart is glad,
and my glory rejoiceth: my flesh also shall rest in hope. . . .
Thou wilt shew me the path of life: in thy presence is
fulness of joy; at thy right hand there are
pleasures for evermore.

Psalm 16: 5-9; 11

He sendeth the springs into the valleys, which run among the hills. They give drink to every beast of the field: the wild asses quench their thirst. By them shall the fowls of the heaven have their habitation, which sing among the branches. He watereth the hills from his chambers: the earth is satisfied with the fruit of thy works. He causeth the grass to grow for the cattle, and herb for the service of man: that he may bring forth food out of the earth; And wine that maketh glad the heart of man, and oil to make his face to shine, and bread which strengtheneth man's heart. The trees of the Lord are full of sap; the cedars of Lebanon, which he hath planted; Where the birds make their nests: as for the stork, the fir trees are her house. The high hills are a refuge for the wild goats; and the rocks for the conies. He appointed the moon for seasons: the sun knoweth his going down. Thou makest darkness, and it is night. . . . The sun ariseth, they gather themselves together, and lay them down in their dens.

Psalm 104: 10-20; 22

*L*ay not up for yourselves treasures

upon earth, where moth and rust

doth corrupt, and where thieves break through and steal:

But lay up for yourselves treasures in heaven,

where neither moth nor rust doth corrupt, and where thieves

do not break through nor steal: For where your treasure is,

there will your heart be also. . . . Therefore I say unto you,

Take no thought for your life, what ye shall eat,

or what ye shall drink; nor yet for your body,

what ye shall put on. Is not the life more than meat,

and the body than raiment?

Behold the fowls of the air: for they sow not,

neither do they reap, nor gather into barns;

yet your heavenly Father feedeth them.

Are ye not much better than they?

Matthew 6: 19-21; 25; 26

How manifold Are Thy Works

GOD'S BEAUTIFUL WORLD

Praise ye the Lord.

Praise God in his sanctuary:

praise him in the firmament of his power.

Praise him for his mighty acts:

praise him according to his excellent greatness.

Praise him with the sound of the trumpet:

praise him with the psaltery and harp.

Praise him with the timbrel and dance:

praise him with stringed instruments and organs.

Praise him upon the loud cymbals:

praise him upon the high sounding cymbals.

Let every thing that hath breath praise the Lord.

Praise ye the Lord.

Psalm 150

To Every Thing
There Is a Season

To every thing
there is
a season,
and a time
to every
purpose under
the heaven.

Ecclesiastes 3: 1

lessed is the man
that walketh not in the counsel
of the ungodly, nor standeth in the way of sinners,
nor sitteth in the seat of the scornful. But his delight
is in the law of the Lord; and in his law doth
he meditate day and night. And he shall be
like a tree planted by the rivers of water,
that bringeth forth his fruit in his season;
his leaf also shall not wither; and
whatsoever he doeth shall prosper.

Psalm 1: 1-3

GOD'S BEAUTIFUL WORLD

Thus saith the Lord God; I will also take of the highest branch of the high cedar, and will set it; I will crop off from the top of his young twigs a tender one, and will plant it upon an high mountain and eminent: In the mountain of the height of Israel will I plant it: and it shall bring forth boughs, and bear fruit, and be a goodly cedar: and under it shall dwell all fowl of every wing; in the shadow of the branches thereof shall they dwell. And all the trees of the field shall know that I the Lord have brought down the high tree, have exalted the low tree, have dried up the green tree, and have made the dry tree to flourish: I the Lord have spoken and have done it.

Ezekiel 17: 22-24

The glory of the Lord shall endure for ever: the Lord shall rejoice in his works. He looketh on the earth, and it trembleth: he toucheth the hills, and they smoke. I will sing unto the Lord as long as I live: I will sing praise to my God while I have my being. My meditation of him shall be sweet: I will be glad in the Lord. Let the sinners be consumed out of the earth, and let the wicked be no more. Bless thou the Lord, O my soul. Praise ye the Lord.

Psalm 104: 31-35

appy is the man that findeth wisdom, and the man that getteth understanding. For the merchandise of it is better than the merchandise of silver, and the gain thereof than fine gold. She is more precious than rubies: and all the things thou canst desire are not to be compared unto her. Length of days is in her right hand; and in her left hand riches and honour. Her ways are ways of pleasantness, and all her paths are peace. She is a tree of life to them that lay hold upon her: and happy is every one that retaineth her.

Proverbs 3: 13-18

ow long wilt thou
forget me, O Lord?
for ever? how long wilt thou hide
thy face from me? How long shall
I take counsel in my soul, having
sorrow in my heart daily? . . .
Consider and hear me, O Lord
my God: lighten mine eyes,
lest I sleep . . . ; Lest mine enemy
say, I have prevailed against him;
and those that trouble me rejoice
when I am moved. But I have trusted
in thy mercy; my heart shall rejoice in
thy salvation. I will sing unto
the Lord, because he hath dealt
bountifully with me.

Psalm 13

*T*o every thing there is a season, and a time to every purpose under the heaven: A time to be born, and a time to die; a time to plant, and a time to pluck up that which is planted; A time to kill, and a time to heal; a time to break down, and a time to build up; A time to weep, and a time to laugh; a time to mourn, and a time to dance; A time to cast away stones, and a time to gather stones together; a time to embrace, and a time to refrain from embracing; A time to get, and a time to lose; a time to keep, and a time to cast away; A time to rend, and a time to sew; a time to keep silence, and a time to speak; A time to love, and a time to hate; a time of war, and a time of peace.

Ecclesiastes 3: 1-8

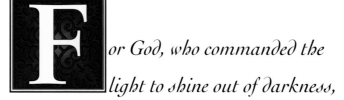

For God, who commanded the

light to shine out of darkness,

hath shined in our hearts, to give the light of the knowledge

of the glory of God in the face of Jesus Christ. But we have this

treasure in earthen vessels, that the excellency of the power

may be of God, and not of us. We are troubled on every side,

yet not distressed; we are perplexed, but not in despair;

Persecuted, but not forsaken; cast down, but not destroyed. . . .

We having the same spirit of faith, according as it is written,

I believed, and therefore have I spoken; we also believe,

and therefore speak; Knowing that he which raised up

the Lord Jesus shall raise up us also by Jesus, and shall

present us with you. For all things are for your sakes,

that the abundant grace might through the thanksgiving of many

redound to the glory of God. . . . While we look not at the things

which are seen, but at the things which are not seen:

for the things which are seen are temporal;

but the things which are not seen are eternal.

II Corinthians 4: 6-9; 13-15; 18

The sun also ariseth, and the sun goeth down,
and hasteth to his place where he arose.
The wind goeth toward the south, and turneth about
unto the north; it whirleth about continually,
and the wind returneth again according to his circuits.
All the rivers run into the sea; yet the sea is not full;
unto the place from whence the rivers come,
thither they return again. All things are full of labour;
man cannot utter it: the eye is not satisfied with seeing,
nor the ear filled with hearing. The thing that hath been,
it is that which shall be; and that which is done
is that which shall be done: and there is
no new thing under the sun.

Ecclesiastes 1: 5-9

Thus saith the Lord; Cursed be the man
that trusteth in man, and maketh flesh his arm,
and whose heart departeth from the Lord. For he shall be
like the heath in the desert, and shall not see when good cometh;
but shall inhabit the parched places in the wilderness,
in a salt land and not inhabited. Blessed is the man that
trusteth in the Lord, and whose hope the Lord is.
For he shall be as a tree planted by the waters, and that
spreadeth out her roots by the river, and shall not see
when heat cometh, but her leaf shall be green;
and shall not be careful in the year of drought,
neither shall cease from yielding fruit.

Jeremiah 17: 5-8

I waited patiently for the Lord; and he inclined unto me, and heard my cry. . . . And he hath put a new song in my mouth, even praise unto our God: many shall see it, and fear, and shall trust in the Lord. Blessed is that man that maketh the Lord his trust, and respecteth not the proud, nor such as turn aside to lies. Many, O Lord my God, are thy wonderful works which thou hast done, and thy thoughts which are to usward: they cannot be reckoned up in order unto thee: if I would declare and speak of them, they are more than can be numbered. . . . Withhold not thou thy tender mercies from me, O Lord: let thy loving kindness and thy truth continually preserve me. . . . Let all those that seek thee rejoice and be glad in thee: let such as love thy salvation say continually, The Lord be magnified. But I am poor and needy; yet the Lord thinketh upon me: thou art my help and my deliverer; make no tarrying, O my God.

Psalm 40: 1; 3-5; 11; 16; 17

I am the true vine, and my Father is the husbandman. Every branch in me that beareth not fruit he taketh away: and every branch that beareth fruit, he purgeth it, that it may bring forth more fruit. Now ye are clean through the word which I have spoken unto you. Abide in me, and I in you. As the branch cannot bear fruit of itself, except it abide in the vine; no more can ye, except ye abide in me. I am the vine, ye are the branches: He that abideth in me, and I in him, the same bringeth forth much fruit: for without me ye can do nothing. If a man abide not in me, he is cast forth as a branch, and is withered; and men gather them, and cast them into the fire, and they are burned. If ye abide in me, and my words abide in you, ye shall ask what ye will, and it shall be done unto you. Herein is my Father glorified, that ye bear much fruit.

John 15: 1-8

**H**ave faith in God.
For verily I say
unto you, That whosoever shall
say unto this mountain,
Be thou removed, and be thou
cast into the sea; and shall
not doubt in his heart,
but shall believe that
those things which he saith
shall come to pass;
he shall have whatsoever
he saith. Therefore I say unto
you, What things soever ye
desire, when ye pray, believe
that ye receive them, and
ye shall have them.

Mark 11: 22-24

Every Thing
Beautiful

He hath made every thing beautiful in his time: also he hath set the world in their heart.

Ecclesiastes 3: 11

Make a joyful noise unto the Lord,
all the earth: make a loud noise,
and rejoice, and sing praise. Sing unto the Lord
with the harp; with the harp, and the voice of a psalm.
With trumpets and sound of cornets make a joyful noise
before the Lord, the King. Let the sea roar, and the fulness
thereof; the world, and they that dwell therein. Let the floods
clap their hands: let the hills be joyful together
Before the Lord; for he cometh to judge the earth:
with righteousness shall he judge the world,
and the people with equity.

Psalm 98: 4-9

Ogive thanks unto
the Lord; call upon his
name: make known his deeds among
the people. Sing unto him,
sing psalms unto him:
talk ye of all his wondrous works.
Glory ye in his holy name:
let the heart of them rejoice
that seek the Lord.
Seek the Lord, and his strength:
seek his face evermore.
Remember his marvellous
works that he hath done;
his wonders, and the judgments
of his mouth.

Psalm 105: 1-5

*O God, my heart is fixed:*

I will sing and give praise,

even with my glory. Awake, psaltery and harp:

I myself will awake early. I will praise thee, O Lord,

among the people: and I will sing praises

unto thee among the nations.

For thy mercy is great above the heavens:

and thy truth reacheth unto the clouds.

Be thou exalted, O God, above the heavens:

and thy glory above all the earth.

Psalm 108: 1-5

Every good gift and every perfect gift is from above, and cometh down from the Father of lights, with whom is no variableness, neither shadow of turning. Of his own will begat he us with the word of truth, that we should be a kind of firstfruits of his creatures. Wherefore, my beloved brethren, let every man be swift to hear, slow to speak, slow to wrath: For the wrath of man worketh not the righteousness of God. . . .For if any be a hearer of the word, and not a doer, he is like unto a man beholding his natural face in a glass: For he beholdeth himself, and goeth his way, and straightway forgetteth what manner of man he was. But whoso looketh into the perfect law of liberty, and continueth therein, he being not a forgetful hearer, but a doer of the work, this man shall be blessed in his deed.

James 1: 17-20; 23-25

GOD'S BEAUTIFUL WORLD

Though I speak with the tongues of men and of angels, and have not charity, I am become as sounding brass, or a tinkling cymbal. And though I have the gift of prophecy, and understand all mysteries, and all knowledge; and though I have all faith, so that I could remove mountains, and have not charity, I am nothing. And though I bestow all my goods to feed the poor, and though I give my body to be burned, and have not charity, it profiteth me nothing. Charity suffereth long, and is kind; charity envieth not; charity vaunteth not itself, is not puffed up, Doth not behave itself unseemly, seeketh not her own, is not easily provoked, thinketh no evil; Rejoiceth not in iniquity, but rejoiceth in the truth; Beareth all things, believeth all things, hopeth all things, endureth all things. Charity never faileth: but whether there be prophecies, they shall fail; whether there be tongues, they shall cease; whether there be knowledge, it shall vanish away. . . .when that which is perfect is come, then that which is in part shall be done away. When I was a child, I spake as a child, I understood as a child, I thought as a child: but when I became a man, I put away childish things. For now we see through a glass, darkly; but then face to face: now I know in part; but then shall I know even as also I am known. And now abideth faith, hope, charity, these three; but the greatest of these is charity.

I Corinthians 13: 1-8; 10-13

He hath made every thing beautiful

in his time: also he hath set the world

in their heart, so that no man can find out the work that

God maketh from the beginning to the end.

I know that there is no good in them,

but for a man to rejoice, and to do

good in his life. And also that every man should eat

and drink, and enjoy the good of all his labour,

it is the gift of God. I know that,

whatsoever God doeth, it shall be for ever:

nothing can be put to it,

nor any thing taken from it.

Ecclesiastes 3: 11-14

*t is a good thing*
to give thanks
unto the Lord, and to sing praises
unto thy name, O most High:
To shew forth thy lovingkindness
in the morning, and thy faithfulness
every night. . . . For thou, Lord,
hast made me glad through
thy work: I will triumph
in the works of thy hands.
O Lord, how great are thy works!
and thy thoughts are very deep.

Psalm 92: 1; 2; 4; 5

 ejoice in the Lord, O ye righteous:
for praise is comely for the upright.
Praise the Lord with harp: sing unto him with the psaltery
and an instrument of ten strings. Sing unto him a
new song; play skilfully with a loud noise. For the word
of the Lord is right; and all his works are done in truth.
He loveth righteousness and judgment: the earth is full
of the goodness of the Lord. By the word of the Lord were
the heavens made; and all the host of them by the breath
of his mouth. He gathereth the waters of the sea together
as an heap: he layeth up the depth in storehouses. . . .
Our soul waiteth for the Lord: he is our help
and our shield. For our heart shall rejoice in him,
because we have trusted in his holy name.
Let thy mercy, O Lord, be upon us,
according as we hope in thee.

Psalm 33: 1-7; 20-22

he Lord is gracious, and full of compassion; slow to anger, and of great mercy. The Lord is good to all: and his tender mercies are over all his works. All thy works shall praise thee, O Lord; and thy saints shall bless thee. They shall speak of the glory of thy kingdom, and talk of thy power; To make known to the sons of men his mighty acts, and the glorious majesty of his kingdom. Thy kingdom is an everlasting kingdom, and thy dominion endureth throughout all generations. The Lord upholdeth all that fall, and raiseth up all those that be bowed down. . . . The Lord is righteous in all his ways, and holy in all his works. The Lord is nigh unto all them that call upon him, to all that call upon him in truth. . . . The Lord preserveth all them that love him. . . . My mouth shall speak the praise of the Lord: and let all flesh bless his holy name for ever and ever.

Psalm 145: 8-14; 17; 18; 20; 21

Praise ye the Lord.
O give thanks unto
the Lord; for he is good: for his mercy
endureth for ever. Who can utter
the mighty acts of the Lord? who can
shew forth all his praise? Blessed are
they that keep judgment, and he
that doeth righteousness at all times.
Remember me, O Lord,
with the favour that thou bearest
unto thy people: O visit me with
thy salvation; That I may see the
good of thy chosen, that I may rejoice
in the gladness of thy nation,
that I may glory with
thine inheritance.

Psalm 106: 1-5

157

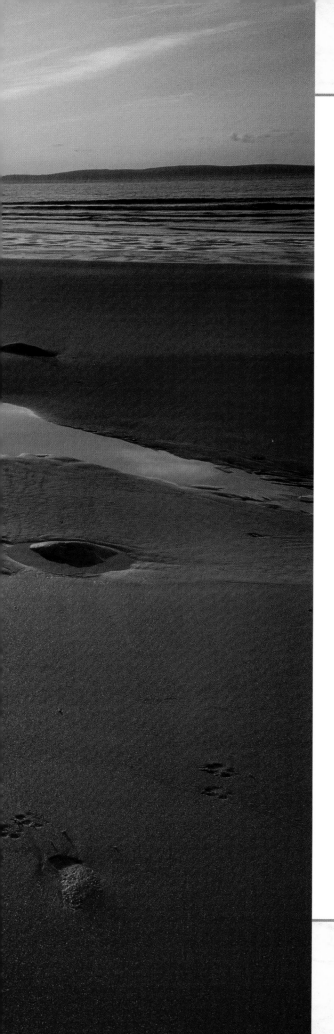

ake a joyful noise unto the Lord, all ye lands. Serve the Lord with gladness: come before his presence with singing. Know ye that the Lord he is God: it is he that hath made us, and not we ourselves; we are his people, and the sheep of his pasture. Enter into his gates with thanksgiving, and into his courts with praise: be thankful unto him, and bless his name. For the Lord is good; his mercy is everlasting; and his truth endureth to all generations.

Psalm 100

A 1
B 2
C 3
D 4
E 5
F 6
G 7
H 8
I 9
J 0